WALES'S LAST DAYS OF COLLIE[

by

Tom Heavyside

Eighteen of the steam locomotives owned by the NCB in Wales at the start of the 1970s had been purchased new after Nationalisation in 1947, the last being accepted in March 1957. Andrew Barclay 0-6-0 side tank works No. 2340, NCB No. 1, seen here at Merthyr Vale Colliery on 6 October 1971, had left the maker's Caledonia Works in Kilmarnock almost eighteen years earlier on 14 December 1953. It had a comparatively short existence, for it was broken up for scrap in August 1975.

Acknowledgements

I would like to record my sincere thanks to Paul Abell, Peter Barber, Bob Darvill, David Dawson, Paul Fox, John Fozard and Eddie Johnson, along with staff at Aberdare Library and the National Coal Mining Museum, Overton, near Wakefield, for their ready help in the compilation of this volume.

Text and photographs © Tom Heavyside, 2011.
First published in the United Kingdom, 2011,
by Stenlake Publishing Ltd.
Telephone: 01290 551122
www.stenlake.co.uk

ISBN 9781840335729

At many locations during the 1970s the NCB relied on the dependable, easily maintained 'Austerity' 0-6-0STs designed by the Hunslet Engine Company of Leeds and released to traffic from 1943. On 1 January 1970 the NCB had twenty-five 'Austerities' on its books in Wales, eleven bought new from Hunslet between 1952 and 1957, the other fourteen purchased second-hand. Here, Hunslet works No. 3840, 'Pamela', which arrived new in South Wales from the manufacturer's Leeds factory in March 1956, has charge of a long rake of wagons while *en route* to Maesteg Central Washery from St John's Colliery on 7 October 1971. St John's is hidden in the fold of the hills behind the train.

Introduction

It is often said, 'South Wales was built on coal'. Undeniably it was the realisation of vast reserves of good quality coal westwards from near the English border to just beyond Llanelli, along with the rapid development of the railway network from the mid-nineteenth century, that radically altered the whole character of the area. Within a comparatively short period of time what were once remote, sparsely populated valleys, in some places picturesque and in others bleak, became transformed into bustling industrial communities with pit-head winding gear and other ancillary colliery buildings dominating the landscape. In the rush to obtain the coal the sides of the valleys quickly became desecrated by vast heaps of discarded waste material, while the once crystal-clear rivers below flowing towards the Bristol Channel became blackened and polluted. Long rows of terraced houses, often perched along the valley sides, were provided for the miners and their families. This transformation wasn't just in the south: not to be overlooked is the much smaller, but nevertheless important coalfield located in much less dramatic terrain in North Wales, not far from the English border.

The meteoric rise of the coal industry in South Wales and the impact it had on life generally can be gleaned from the fact that during the early 1850s the area yielded approximately eight and a half million tons of coal each year from a labour force totalling almost 30,000. Sixty years later, in 1913, over fifty-six million tons was realised, the employees having increased to over 250,000. Meanwhile a number of large dock complexes had been developed along the north coast of the Bristol Channel to cater for the lucrative export trade, a seemingly never-ending procession of wagons weaving their way along the valleys *en route* between the pits and ports.

In the event 1913 proved the zenith of the coal industry, for due to the combined effects of the First World War, when many overseas markets were lost, and the harsh economic conditions that prevailed during the 1920s and 1930s, output fell rapidly. Some of the more uneconomic pits inevitably fell by the wayside while many local concerns lost their identity, their assets merged into one of the larger combines such as Powell Duffryn Ltd and Partridge, Jones & John Paton Ltd, amalgamations encouraged by the government as a means of increasing efficiency.

Such was the decline of the coal industry that by 1947, when the industry came under state ownership following Nationalisation, total output in South Wales had fallen to 25,800,000 tons. Even so, over 104,000 men in the region, employed at 195 collieries, were still reliant on the mines for their weekly pay packet. But despite the National Coal Board investing heavily in many of the pits during the 1950s and 1960s, the run-down of the industry continued unabated. This was due to a variety of reasons, including the increasing use of cheap oil as an alternative fuel and the implementation of smoke control orders under the Clean Air Act of 1956. Thus, at the beginning of January 1970 the number of collieries in South Wales had been brought down to sixty-one, with a much reduced workforce.

These colliery closures, along with the introduction of diesel locomotives at some outlets, inevitably impacted on the ranks of the NCB's steam locomotives in South Wales, a fleet in excess of 180 in 1947 being reduced to seventy-three at the start of January 1970. The latter included five operated by the NCB Coal Products Division and three by the Opencast Executive. Surprisingly, the steam stock owned in 1970 had emanated from no less than thirteen independent locomotive factories, including ten constructed prior to the First World War, the oldest in 1900, while thirty-eight were comparatively modern machines dating from the 1940s and 1950s, the youngest having been outshopped in 1957. Sixty-six carried their water supplies in a saddle tank, thirteen with a 0-4-0 and fifty-three with a 0-6-0 wheel configuration. Two were 0-6-0 side tanks while the remaining five were ex-Great Western Railway 0-6-0 pannier tanks bought second-hand by the NCB from British Railways. In 1970 the steam stud was dispersed between thirty-one locations.

Meanwhile in North Wales, of the seven operational mines acquired by the NCB in 1947 (total sales 1,962,500 tons, employees 7,950) only three remained in 1970, the numerical strength of the steam locomotives in the area having been reduced from ten to six during the intervening period. This select sextet, allocated between Bersham and Gresford collieries, near Wrexham, had each been built by a different manufacturer and consisted of two 0-4-0STs, three 0-6-0STs and one 0-6-0T. The oldest had been built back in 1890, the youngest in 1945.

Mainly due to further colliery closures the dependence on steam locomotives diminished further throughout the 1970s, so that by the end of the decade only twenty-one were listed on the asset register of the NCB in Wales, nineteen based in the south and two in the north. However, the arrival of diesel locomotives at Bersham Colliery in January 1980 spelt the end of steam in the north. Regular steam working also came to an end in the south that year when the fireboxes were cleaned out for the last time at Brynlliw Colliery, Grovesend, the coal stocking site at Pontardulais, and at Mountain Ash. After that only Peckett 0-6-0ST works No. 1889, 'Menelaus', built in 1934, based at Marine Colliery, Cwm, Ebbw Vale, remained available for use, although it was very seldom called upon. There was a last ceremonial steaming of 'Menelaus' at Marine on 28 June 1985.

During the 1980s the NCB disposed of all its remaining steam locomotives in Wales, either for scrap or to the burgeoning railway preservation movement. The last loco to leave, Hunslet 'Austerity' 0-6-0ST works No. 3840, 'Pamela', built in 1956, departed Maesteg for a new life on 16 June 1986. In fact, no less than thirty-four of the NCB steam locomotives domiciled in Wales in 1970 have been preserved, twelve still residing in the country with the rest located much further afield, ranging from Brechin, near Montrose in Scotland, to Cornwall, Hampshire and Essex in the south of England.

By the 1980s what few collieries still survived were also nearing the end. The last to close in North Wales was Point of Ayr Colliery, on the coastline near Prestatyn, on 23 August 1996. In the south of the country the celebrated Tower Colliery, Hirwaun, north of Aberdare, lasted until 25 January 2008, although this was entirely due to an employee buy-out scheme in 1994, following the privatisation of the industry, when 239 men contributed £8,000 each in order to keep the mine operative. Today, only a few opencast sites remain active, but compared to times past these have very little influence on the economy of the country.

With the demise of the traditional methods of mining many places are now far more environmentally friendly than they have been for decades, this being particularly noticeable in the South Wales valleys. Apart from a few notable exceptions, the once prominent colliery winding gear mechanisms above the shafts have been dismantled and the related buildings demolished, while many of the unsightly spoil heaps have been removed or grassed over. Nature has once more been allowed to take its course, even salmon and trout having been enticed back to their old haunts by the purer water that now flows from the hillsides into the rivers.

But while radical changes have taken place in the former coalfields, the rich heritage of the past has not been forgotten. Major museums devoted to the coal mining industry have been established, including those at the former Lewis Merthyr Colliery, Trehafod, (known as the Rhondda Heritage Park), at Big Pit, Blaenavon, and at Cefn Coed Colliery, Crynant, near Neath. Throughout the country many local reminders of the past in the form of monuments and plaques can be seen at old colliery sites. Perhaps most poignant of all is the large earth sculpture 'Sultan the Pit Pony' near Ystrad Mynach, a symbol that marks the transformation of the Valleys and the end of an era.

Remembering those heady days of the 1970s, the collieries in North Wales were conveniently located just over an hour's drive away from my Lancashire home, while visiting the pits in South Wales were more of a minor expedition, although the long journeys invariably proved worthwhile. To quote but two examples, I will never forget the spectacle of the seemingly incessant shunting that took place near the town centre of Mountain Ash, the bridge across the valley doubling as a convenient grandstand for what some might argue was the greatest free show on earth. So, too, will I always remember descending the mountain road from Aberdare for the first time and, as the town of Maerdy came into view, witnessing the evocative sight of the 'Mardy Monster' at work in the vast exchange sidings spread across the floor of the Rhondda Fach. Furthermore, wherever I went the welcome was always warm and friendly, with footplate rides on occasions being freely offered. Happy days indeed!

Between 1951 and 1965 the NCB purchased from British Railways twelve locomotives to Great Western Railway designs for use in South Wales. This is Class 57XX 0-6-0 pannier tank No. 7754 at Mountain Ash, four miles south-east of Aberdare, on 5 October 1971. Constructed for the GWR by the North British Locomotive Company at its Queen's Park Works, Glasgow, in 1930, it had 17½in. x 24in. inside cylinders, 4ft 7½in. wheels, and in full working order weighed 47 tons 10cwt. Initially based at Reading shed and then Southall, it moved to Old Oak Common, London, in June 1935 where it stayed nearly fourteen years. Under BR ownership it was reallocated to Wellington, Shropshire, in April 1949, being withdrawn from there in January 1959 with a recorded mileage of 580,990. It was sold to the NCB the following July, seeing service at five NCB locations before moving to Mountain Ash from Talywain in May 1970. No. 7754 lay idle from 1975 before being vested in the Welsh Industrial & Maritime Museum in 1980, the engine immediately being placed on permanent loan with the Llangollen Railway in North Wales.

The United Westminster & Wrexham Collieries Ltd started preliminary work on the sinking of Gresford Colliery, two miles north-east of Wrexham, during autumn 1907. Five years later, in 1912, the shafts were completed to a maximum depth of 2,263 feet. The company maintained the pit until it relinquished ownership to the National Coal Board at the start of 1947. That year the colliery raised 452,500 tons of coal for gas, household and steam purposes with 1,830 men being listed on the payroll, 1,460 working below ground and 370 on the surface.

The internal shunting at Gresford was always the preserve of steam locomotives and here on 5 June 1972 Robert Stephenson & Hawthorns 'Austerity' 0-6-0ST works No. 7135, 'Gwyneth', built in 1944, returns light engine from the BR exchange sidings to the colliery yard. The connecting line between the sidings and the Chester–Shrewsbury route is visible behind 'Gwyneth', as is the main line to the right of the exhaust.

The engine was one of ninety 'Austerities' built at the maker's Newcastle-upon-Tyne factory between 1943 and 1945 to a Hunslet design for the Ministry of Supply to assist the war effort, both on the home front and overseas. As WD (War Department) No. 75185 it was shipped to France in May 1945 and, later, after a period in storage at Calais, returned home in 1947. Almost immediately it was sold to the NCB for use at Llay Main Colliery, near Wrexham, where it was named 'Gwyneth'. When Llay Main closed in 1966 it was moved the short distance to Gresford where it remained until transported to the NCB Walkden Central Workshops, near Manchester, in April 1974. After a complete overhaul it saw further service at Bickershaw Colliery, Leigh, Lancashire. Later, following withdrawal at Bickershaw, many of its major components – boiler, cylinders, etc. – were salvaged to assist in the creation of a replica Great Western Railway broad gauge (7ft 0¼in.) locomotive, 'Iron Duke', for the National Railway Museum at York in 1985.

The two engines depicted here dumped outside the engine shed at Gresford on 21 August 1973 both look in a somewhat sorry state. They had originally emanated from near neighbours based in Leeds, the 0-6-0T 'Richboro' (nearest the camera) from Hudswell Clarke in 1917, their works No. 1243, and the 0-6-0ST from Hunslet in 1945, their works no. 3206. The latter, former WD No. 71442 and built to the renowned wartime Austerity design with 18in. diameter and 26in. stroke inside cylinders and 4ft 3in. diameter wheels, had been based here since 1962. As regards the slightly smaller 'Richboro', fitted with 16in. x 24in. outside cylinders and 3ft 9in. wheels, this was supplied on completion to the Inland Waterways and Docks Authority at Richborough, near Ramsgate, Kent. It was sold to Ifton Colliery, St Martin's, near Gobowen, Shropshire, around 1926, where it remained until its transfer to Gresford in 1969. Happily 'Richboro' still survives, although far away from its roots at the Bo'ness & Kinneil Railway in Scotland. The remains of the 'Austerity' were disposed of in August 1977.

On the same day as the previous photograph, Hunslet 'Austerity' 0-6-0ST 'Alison' runs slowly through the spacious yard at Gresford. When new in April 1944, the engine, as works No. 3163, was forwarded from the maker's Jack Lane factory in Leeds to the War Department's Bicester depot in Oxfordshire. After a varied army career as WD No. 75113 it was repurchased by Hunslet in October 1962 and given a complete rebuild and a new works number, 3885, in 1964. Unfortunately the engine proved difficult to sell, and except for a loan spell of one year to Coventry Homefire Plant from May 1965, it remained stored at Leeds until July 1970 when it was sold to the NCB North Western Area. After attention at Walkden Central Workshops it arrived at Gresford in November 1970, where it acquired the name 'Alison'. Sadly, by the date of this photograph there was little life left in the colliery, the last coal being brought up the shafts on 10 November 1973. The buildings were subsequently erased, a small industrial estate now covering the site, although nearby a winding wheel forms part of a memorial unveiled by HRH Prince Charles on 26 November 1982 which recalls Gresford's darkest day when 266 men lost their lives on 22 September 1934 due to an explosion underground. Meanwhile 'Alison' was transferred to Bold Colliery, St Helens, Lancashire, in April 1974. It is currently resident on the East Lancashire Railway at Bury, but carrying the name 'Sapper', as it did for a short time during its army days.

Opposite: The sinking of Bersham Colliery at Rhostyllen, two miles south-west of Wrexham, began in 1868, although it was not until 1879 that the shafts reached their maximum depth of 1,266 feet. Like Gresford, the pit was conveniently located by the ex-Great Western Railway Chester–Shrewsbury line, seen in the foreground of the photograph. Here, as the shunter looks on anxiously, Hawthorn Leslie 0-4-0ST 'Shakespeare' – constructed at the maker's Forth Banks Works, Newcastle-upon-Tyne, in 1914 as works No. 3072 – pulls a set of loaded wagons away from the screens on 17 September 1979. On the right a line of empties await their turn to be filled. The engine's first home was the ill-fated Shakespeare Cliff Colliery, near Dover, hence its name, and when that venture was abandoned in December 1915 it was requisitioned by the Ministry of Munitions. Later it was acquired by local dealers Cudworth & Johnson who, around 1928, hired it to Bersham where its four-coupled 3ft 6in. wheels and short wheelbase proved well-suited to the sharp curves at this restricted site, so much so that it was purchased outright shortly afterwards.

With Bersham Sidings signal box and a lower quadrant signal in the off position in readiness for the passage of a southbound train on the right, Peckett Class W6 0-4-0ST works No. 1935, 'Hornet', built in 1937, propels six loaded wagons from the headshunt on 5 June 1972. Like the rest of the class the engine has 14in. x 22in. outside cylinders and 3ft 2½in. wheels, but it was specially adapted at Peckett's Atlas Locomotive Works, Bristol, with the cab floor positioned lower than the frames for work at Black Park Colliery, Chirk, because of restricted clearances. The unusual chimney is the remnant of an unauthorised American wood-burning smokestack type that replaced the original squat version while at Ifton Colliery, St Martin's, before the engine was reallocated to Bersham in November 1968. Today the unusual design features of this locomotive can be studied at the Ribble Steam Railway, Preston.

During the 1970s the average output at Bersham amounted to 193,000 tons per annum, most of it destined for the British Steel Corporation Plant at Shotton, between Chester and Flint. During this same decade, as a result of increased productivity, the number of men employed at the colliery fell from 760 to 550. On 21 August 1973 the veteran 'Shakespeare' stands by as relative youngster BR Type 2 Class 25 Bo-Bo diesel-electric locomotive No. 5287 (later No. 25137), released from Derby Works in 1964, returns empty wagons from Shotton. Ironically, the diesel was withdrawn from service in October 1980 after a life of only sixteen years, one month before 'Shakespeare' met its end at the hands of a scrap merchant in November of the same year.

On the same day, with the cast nameplate prominent on the side of the saddle tank and the shunter riding on the footplate steps, 'Shakespeare' hauls a couple of rather decrepit wooden wagons from the landsale area. Needless to say, these wagons were only used within the confines of the colliery. The steam locomotives at Bersham became redundant at the start of 1980, when diesels took over after some of the tight curves at the colliery had been eased. However this was not for very long – with the reserves exhausted, the miners returned to the surface for the last time on 18 December 1986. Small businesses now occupy the buildings, renamed as Bersham Enterprise Park, and the most prominent reminders of the past are the retention of the headgear above one of the shafts and the large spoil heap.

The area around Blaenavon, some seven miles north of Pontypool in South Wales, was rich in coal and ironstone reserves, the seams being conveniently located at comparatively shallow levels. In 1789 three blast furnaces were blown, heralding the beginning of what became a vast industrial complex that eventually included, in addition to the coal and ironstone workings, limestone quarries, coke ovens, steelworks, brickworks and a rail rolling mill. By the 1870s the Blaenavon Iron & Steel Company owned no less than sixteen coal mines, although only three survived long enough to become owned by the NCB in 1947. By 1970 only the shafts at Big Pit (sunk in 1860), which reached a maximum depth of 293 feet, were still in use, although from 1973 the coal was brought to the surface by means of a new drift. Pictured here, shunting the sidings at the nearby Blaenavon Coal Preparation Plant on 22 May 1973, is Andrew Barclay 0-4-0ST works No. 1619, which started its career here when new in March 1919. It had 16in. x 24in. cylinders, 3ft 7in. wheels and rather cumbersome cast nameplates on the side of the saddle tank – 'The Blaenavon Toto No. 6'. 'Toto' was the name of a former manager's dog. Confusingly, from 1961 the loco carried the wrong maker's identification plates, those belonging to a fellow Andrew Barclay 0-4-0ST, works No. 1502, built in 1917, which had been bought by the NCB for spare parts from the old Blaenavon Company the previous year. Presumably, the cab from the latter was in much better condition than that on 'Toto', but when the exchange was made no one bothered to refit the correct works plates.

Later the same day, 'The Blaenavon Toto No. 6' stands impatiently in front of the screens at Blaenavon while awaiting its next move. Diesels superseded steam here for the last three years of the plant's existence before Big Pit closed in February 1980. Since then the town of Blaenavon, which has many buildings from the early days of the iron and coal industries still standing, has become a major tourist attraction and designated a UNESCO World Heritage Site. Big Pit has been preserved as a mining museum with underground tours available, while nearby the Pontypool & Blaenavon Railway operates heritage steam and diesel locomotives along a section of the former London & North Western Railway Brynmawr to Abersychan & Talywain route. The steam locomotive depicted here also lives on, but now in Essex at the Mangapps Railway at Burnham-on-Crouch.

Four miles from Blaenavon down the Avon-Iwyd Valley, the engine shed at Talywain once maintained the motive power required for the tortuous, steeply inclined two and a half mile branch to the isolated Blaenserchan Colliery. For a long number of years the miners were transported to their workplace by 'Paddy' trains, latterly consisting of old BR fruit vans adapted with bench seats and handbrakes, timed to coincide with the start and end of each shift. The line to Blaenserchan was closed on 3 April 1970 when the colliery output was diverted underground via Tirpentwys Colliery to Hafodyrynys Colliery, near Pontypool, where it reached the surface. After that there was still a need for locomotives at Talywain, but simply to service the adjacent landsale yard, a job often completed in about two hours. Two identical Andrew Barclay 0-6-0STs, built new for the NCB in 1952, were retained for this duty, works No. 2331 'Illtyd', which was never employed anywhere else, and works No. 2332 'Islwyn', which arrived from Tirpentwys Colliery after winding ceased there in September 1959. They had 17in. x 24in. cylinders and 3ft 7in. wheels. The former was named after the founder of a monastery at Llantwit, while Islwyn was an eminent Monmouthshire poet. Latterly 'Illtyd' was used as a source of spare parts to help keep its companion serviceable. 'Islwyn' is pictured here on 21 May 1973 (the day all the photographs at Talywain included here were taken), outside the shed being prepared for duty. On the right the discarded firebox, boiler and smokebox which were formerly fitted to Hunslet 'Austerity' 0-6-0ST works No. 3817, 'Llewellyn', built in 1954 (see page 19), lie derelict. On the left is the old granary, once used as a grain store for the pit ponies, while behind, at a higher level, can be seen a number of miners' cottages.

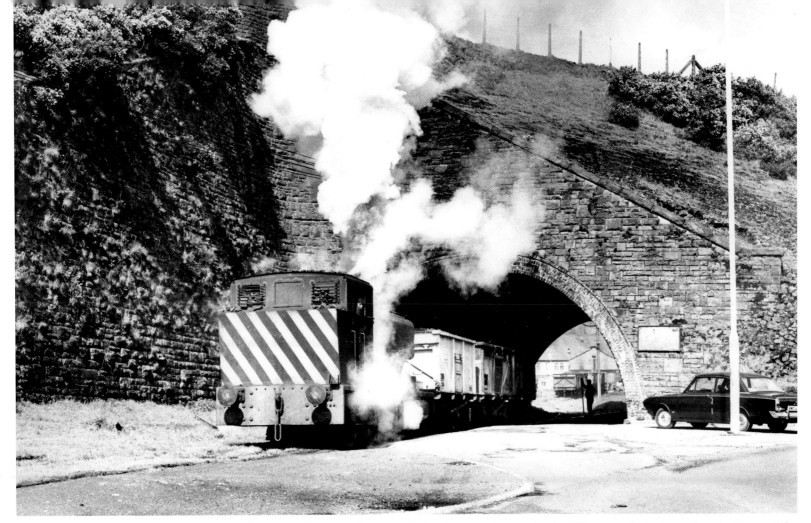

'Islwyn' pushes a few wagons under Big Arch towards the landsale yard at Talywain as the driver of a Ford Corsair waits for it to clear. Just beyond the arch the latcher – as he was known in these parts – with his shunting pole ready at hand, takes advantage of a moment's respite. The shed can be seen in the background. High overhead were the tracks of the former Great Western Railway branch from Newport. At one time the tracks leading from the depot extended a further half mile or so down the valley where they connected with the GWR line at Pentwyn Junction, but by this time the truncated remains merely provided a headshunt for the yard.

Leaking steam from a number of places where it shouldn't, 'Islwyn' exerts every ounce of its strength while dragging six empty wagons, destined for the exchange sidings, up the ferocious incline away from the landsale yard at Talywain. At the bottom of the bank the rails can be seen veering to the left towards the headshunt under Big Arch. The telegraph poles high on the embankment on the extreme left of the picture mark the route of the ex-GWR lines, tracks which became jointly owned with the London & North Western Railway near where I was standing to take this photograph, before becoming the sole property of the LNWR another half mile further on. A number of narrow gauge wagons can be identified in the compound to the right of 'Islwyn'. Blaenserchan Colliery is hidden by the hills to the left of the photograph.

Observed from the same vantage point a few seconds later, 'Islwyn' continues its laborious battle against the gradient. Soon it will reach the point where the line starts to curve almost through 180 degrees to reach the site of the long-closed Navigation Colliery. From there it will reverse its load around another equally long curve in order to gain Castle Pond exchange sidings, adjacent to the abandoned platforms of the former Abersychan & Talywain station, from which passenger services were withdrawn back in 1941.

With the hard work over and 'Islwyn' now in reverse gear, the driver has time to admire the scenery as the wagons are guided slowly from the former Navigation Colliery site to Castle Pond sidings. The name, stencilled in small letters on the side of the cab, can just be discerned through a thick layer of grime. The last consignment of coal was collected from the landsale yard at Talywain in June 1974, with both 'Islwyn' and 'Illtyd' being scrapped on site in July of the following year.

Hafodyrynys New Mine, a level drift three miles west of Pontypool, was constructed between 1954 and 1959 at a cost of over £5 million; the original colliery, completed in 1914, was owned prior to Nationalisation by Crumlin Valley Collieries Ltd, a subsidiary of Partridge, Jones & John Paton Ltd. In 1960 the new washery processed 488,000 tons of coal, although this included 130,000 tons raised at the nearby Glyntillery Colliery and 171,000 tons from Tirpentwys Colliery which had been connected underground to the new drift. Pictured here at the eastern end of the site on a dank 4 October 1971, Hunslet 'Austerity' 0-6-0ST works No. 3810, 'Glendower', built in 1954, is coupled to a motley array of NCB internal user wagons. The track on the south side of the valley, known as the Glyn Railway, once served other local collieries but latterly was used simply for the disposal of prodigious amounts of waste material. The full wagons in the foreground await collection by BR. They will depart eastwards from the sidings towards Pontypool along the remaining stub of the former GWR line that until June 1964 had formed part of a through route to Neath via Mountain Ash. Today, 'Glendower' is based on the South Devon Railway at Buckfastleigh, near Totnes.

On a much brighter day at Hafodyrynys, 21 May 1973, Hunslet 'Austerity' 0-6-0ST works No. 3817, 'Llewellyn', which like 'Glendower' was built in 1954, looks a little forlorn (as do some of the wagons) standing near the gigantic spoil bunker. The waste was carried to the tipping grounds alongside the former Glyn Railway in side-discharge wagons, one of which can be seen nearest the camera behind 'Llewellyn'. The engine had arrived from Talywain about eighteen months earlier after the boiler had been replaced by that previously carried by another Hafodyrynys resident, Hunslet 'Austerity' works No. 3780, 'Gwent', built in 1952. Once the wagons under the screens on the right were fully loaded, the brakes would be released allowing them to run by gravity onto the traverser, seen in the foreground. They would then be transferred to the appropriate siding, out of sight to the left of the picture, according to their destination, a most unusual arrangement at a colliery. The colliery closed at the end of December 1975, although the washery continued until January 1978, with the last coal stocks being removed in March of the following year. The re-aligned A472 road from Pontypool now passes through the site, although the round washery building on the extreme right-hand side of the picture still stands, albeit looking a little forlorn. 'Llewellyn' was scrapped earlier during the summer of 1976.

At Tymawr Colliery, Trehafod, near Pontypridd in the Rhondda, Glamorganshire, Peckett Class W5 0-4-0ST works No. 1676, built in 1925, is seen at the landsale yard on a somewhat damp 23 May 1973, the day this and the photographs on the next two pages were taken. Near the far end of the line of wagons a merchant is bagging and loading coal onto a lorry ready for delivery to local households; nearer the camera, the shunter attends to the dropped side of an already emptied wooden wagon. Above the wagons on the right an upturned bucket descends the aerial ropeway after depositing waste on the tip, while just above the second wagon behind the locomotive a loaded bucket begins yet another climb to the tipping site. On the left can be seen the winding wheel above one of the shafts. Locomotives were not used at Tymawr until 1960 when it merged with Lewis Merthyr Colliery, the coal from both workings subsequently being hoisted to the surface at Tymawr. After working at Lewis Merthyr from new in 1925, No. 1676 made the short journey to Tymawr in 1964.

Here the Peckett pushes a BR standard 16-ton capacity mineral wagon around the unkempt yard. One of literally thousands of such wagons, this example was built by Metropolitan-Cammell Carriage & Wagon Company of Birmingham in 1955. The contents could be released either by way of a dropped side door or the hinged end, identified by the faded diagonal stripe on the body side.

The driver and shunter seem intent on shovelling as much coal as possible into the bunker of Peckett works No. 1676. As built, the Class W5s had a very limited coal carrying capacity and the bunker was a later modification. Some coal has spilled onto the footplate. The identification number 1676 has been rather crudely chalked on the side of the cab where the maker's cast identification plate was originally affixed.

No. 1676 drags fellow 0-4-0ST, NCB No. 31, which is nearest the camera with its smokebox door slightly ajar, around the yard at Tymawr. No. 31 was created by an amalgam of parts from three engines at Marine Colliery, Cwm, south of Ebbw Vale, in 1967 and 1968. Components from two Peckett Class Es were utilised, works No. 1465 'Sir Charles Allen' and No. 1524 'King George V', which had 15in. x 21in. outside cylinders and 3ft 7in. wheels, and were originally bought by the Ebbw Vale Steel, Iron & Coal Co. Ltd in 1917 and 1919 respectively. The third engine involved, No. 2 'Nasmyth', was built by the Ebbw Vale Company themselves in 1907, one of eight they put together between 1905 and 1917. 'Nasmyth' had the same dimensions as the Class Es, the Bristol company supplying many of the components. The resultant No. 31 was slightly larger than its companion (No. 1676 had 14in. x 20in. cylinders and 3ft 2½in. wheels), but the similarity in the design of the two engines and the Peckett pedigree of No. 31 is readily apparent. No. 31 had only arrived at Tymawr a few days before this photograph was taken, coming from Hafodyrynys Colliery where it had spent the previous four years. It never turned a wheel in anger at Tymawr, being broken up for scrap along with No. 1676 during April 1976.

Seven years later when the final tub of coal was brought from below ground it was suitably inscribed, 'The Last Dram of Coal Tymawr Colliery June 21 1983' along with the names of the hitcher, banksman, winder and deputy electrician. The site was later developed for housing, while the nearby Lewis Merthyr Colliery was subsequently transformed into the Rhondda Heritage Park, a lasting tribute to the proud traditions of the coal industry. There are other reminders of the past in the area, notably at Rhondda Golf Club, Penrhys, where each hole is named after a local colliery. Lewis Merthyr is the tenth hole while appropriately the eighteenth is Mardy, this being the last mine in the Rhondda to close (see page 37).

Four miles south of Merthyr Tydfil, Merthyr Vale Colliery, located in the village of the same name, first went into production under the direction of Nixon Taylor & Cory in 1875. The mine became owned by Nixon's Navigation Co. Ltd in 1882, and then Llewellyn (Nixon) Ltd from 1929, before becoming part of the Powell Duffryn empire in 1936. Under the direction of the NCB the pit produced 350,000 tons of coal and employed 1,082 men in 1947, although by the 1970s output had reduced to 250,000 tons per annum and the number of employees to 600. Sadly, the colliery will always be associated with the horrific disaster of 21 October 1966, when waste that had been dumped over the years high on the hillside above suddenly slipped, engulfing the local Aberfan primary school and resulting in the loss of 144 lives including 116 children.

Here, with the River Taff on the left and the village of Aberfan beyond, Andrew Barclay 0-6-0T works No. 2340, NCB No. 1, built in 1953, propels some freshly hewn coal along the three-quarter mile branch from the colliery to Black Lion exchange sidings on 6 October 1971. The colliery headgear can be discerned on the extreme right-hand side of the picture, while in the foreground is the ex-Taff Vale Railway Cardiff–Merthyr Tydfil line. In the immediate foreground is the trackbed (now a heritage trail) of the historic Penydarren to Abercynon tramroad, along which the first steam locomotive to run on rails, built by Richard Trevithick, hauled 10 tons of iron and numerous passengers on 21 February 1804.

No. 1 first came to Merthyr Vale in October 1965 after reallocation from the NCB Aberaman Railway, where it had been since new in December 1953. It had 18in. x 24in. outside cylinders and 3ft 9in. wheels. Apart from a short sojourn of about nine months from the spring of 1966 at Mardy Colliery, the engine stayed at Merthyr Vale for the rest of its days. It was dismantled on site for scrap some time after July 1975.

On the same day as the previous photograph, No. 1 is about to pass over the level crossing on the B4285 road (visible on the left) as it hauls yet more coal away from Merthyr Vale Colliery. The landsale yard is on the right, and the houses above are by the main A470 Cardiff–Brecon road.

Again on 6 October 1971, Peckett Class OX3 0-6-0ST works No. 2061, NCB No. 6, has charge of three wagons at Merthyr Vale. The leading wagon is marked for loco coal. The car ascending the B4285 road on the right has just passed over the level crossing. No. 6 was originally supplied to Slough Estates Ltd in February 1945 before becoming the property of the NCB in 1949. Following spells on the Aberaman and Mountain Ash systems it was moved to Merthyr Vale shortly after it had been rebuilt by W.G. Bagnall Ltd at their Castle Engine Works, Stafford, in 1962. The outside cylinders measured 16in. x 24in. and the wheels 3ft 10in. No. 6 faced the acetylene torch in the yard of scrap metal dealers W.J. Harris & Sons, near Pontypool Road station, in January 1975. Coal was last lifted from the seams below Merthyr Vale on 25 August 1989 and the area has since been landscaped.

From the mid 1860s the Mountain Ash Railway in the Cynon Valley, and its related collieries, were under the same ownership as Merthyr Vale Colliery (see page 23). The colliery lines were sandwiched between the ex-Great Western Railway Pontypool–Neath line and, on the opposite side of the river, the former Taff Vale Railway Cardiff–Aberdare route. BR withdrew the passenger services from both lines in 1964, only the old Taff Vale metals being retained for freight traffic. Despite the presence of diesels, the NCB continued to utilise steam locomotives at Mountain Ash throughout the 1970s, the engine shed and workshop facilities being conveniently situated close to the centre of the town.

Seen here from the road overbridge that links the two sides of the valley at Mountain Ash, Avonside 0-6-0ST works No. 1680, 'Sir John', passes ex-GWR 0-6-0PT No. 7754 as it makes a spirited getaway with a long link of mainly empty wagons on 5 October 1971. 'Sir John' is about to travel north over the tracks of the old GWR line, these having been taken over by the NCB early in 1971 principally to provide a direct link with Aberaman Phurnacite Plant further up the valley. The engine shed and workshops, along with the headgear of the 1967-closed Abergorki Colliery, are visible through the haze beyond the pannier tank, while the overgrown platforms of the closed Mountain Ash Cardiff Road station can be seen above the leading two wagons behind 'Sir John'. The Afon Cynon is shielded from view by the trees on the right.

'Sir John' was originally delivered from the maker's Fishponds works, Bristol, to the WD Tidworth Camp, Hampshire, in 1914. It arrived at Mountain Ash in November 1929 after purchase by Llewellyn (Nixon) Ltd. Its 3ft 3in. wheels were powered by 14in. x 20in. cylinders. The rather plain-looking chimney had been fabricated from an old methane gas pipe in the Mountain Ash workshops, after the original had been irreparably damaged under the screens at Deep Duffryn Colliery.

A pair of 0-6-0STs, Peckett works No. 1859 'Sir Gomer' (nearest the camera) and Hudswell Clarke works No. 1885, NCB No. 1, built in 1932 and 1955 respectively, enjoy a moment of quiet, as do the drivers outside the two-road shed at Mountain Ash on 26 May 1973. The road overbridge from which the previous photograph was taken can be seen on the left, with the winding gear at Deep Duffryn Colliery protruding above.

The close proximity of the colliery lines to the town centre of Mountain Ash is apparent as Andrew Barclay 0-6-0ST works No. 2074 pauses briefly at the entrance to Deep Duffryn Colliery on a damp and dismal 23 May 1973. A branch of Lloyds Bank occupies a strategic position on the corner of Commercial Street, leading to Aberdare, and Pryce Street. Motorists heading across the bridge for Penrhiwceiber (one mile away) needed to turn left at the junction, down Oxford Street. The Gas Board is housed in the two-storey building on the left while the Town Hall is directly behind the position from where I took the photograph. The Afon Cynon flows beneath the stone arch to be seen above the cab of the loco.

After completion at the manufacturer's Kilmarnock factory in 1939, the engine made the long journey south to the nearby Penrikyber Colliery at Penrhiwceiber. Its 3ft 5in. wheels are powered by 14in. x 22in. outside cylinders. It was named after 'Llantarnam Abbey' in Monmouthshire, originally the site of a medieval Cistercian Monastery, but in more recent years occupied by the Sisters of St Joseph. The engine first moved to Mountain Ash in September 1957, but was later transferred to Merthyr Vale Colliery and then the Aberaman Railway, before returning in 1964. In 1971 it travelled north to the NCB workshops at Walkden, near Manchester, where after an overhaul and a fresh coat of green paint the name was wrongly applied as 'Llantanam Abbey', i.e. without the letter 'r' as seen here. The error was rectified in later years.

Opposite: Photographed the previous day from a position opposite Lloyds Bank, Robert Stephenson & Hawthorns 'Austerity' 0-6-0ST works No. 7139, NCB No. 8, built in 1944, shunts loaded wagons from Deep Duffryn Colliery towards the abandoned platforms of Mountain Ash Oxford Street (ex-Taff Vale Railway) station. In its earlier days as WD No. 75189 the locomotive enjoyed an army career that lasted sixteen years, before it was disposed of to the Hunslet Engine Company of Leeds in 1960. After a complete rebuild as Hunslet works No. 3880, it was resold the following year to the NCB for use at Mountain Ash. The shiny rails at the bottom left-hand corner of the frame lead to Aberdare, while the track straddling the Afon Cynon on the right connected with the former GWR side of the complex. Deep Duffryn Colliery, sunk in 1850 and the oldest working colliery in South Wales at the time, yielded 230,000 tons of coal per annum during the early 1970s and employed 580 men. The shafts reached a depth of 1,227 feet.

Left: South of Mountain Ash, Peckett Class OX1 0-6-0ST works No. 1859, 'Sir Gomer', bought new by Llewellyn (Nixon) Ltd in June 1932, draws away from the coal stocking site on 22 May 1973. The engine had 16in. x 24in. cylinders and 3ft 10in. wheels. Peckett's supplied a new boiler, smokebox, copper firebox and brass tubes for the engine in November 1953. It acquired a further new boiler during a protracted eighteen-month visit to the NCB workshops at Walkden from June 1971, before returning in December 1972. The engine took its name from Sir Gomer Berry, a Merthyr-born industrialist and newspaper proprietor. This section of line assumed even more importance from 1974, when a little lower down the valley a conveyor was erected to carry coal from Penrikyber Colliery, Penrhiwceiber, to a new loading bunker on this side of the river. This enabled the NCB to transport the output from Penrikyber to Deep Duffryn for washing and onwards to Aberaman Phurnacite Plant without the need to rely on BR as previously. At the time the conveyor was commissioned Penrikyber was lifting from below ground some 272,000 tons of coal per annum, with some 860 men relying on the pit for their weekly wage packet.

Right: The seemingly insatiable demands of the Aberaman Phurnacite Plant, one mile north of Mountain Ash, meant the railway had to operate seven days a week. Photographed on Sunday 28 March 1976, overlooked by the backs of properties on Oxford Street, 'Sir Gomer' passes through Mountain Ash with coal mined at Penrikyber Colliery. On the right the substantial 1974-built weighbridge office stands on the trackbed of the old GWR Pontypool–Neath line. By this time there was little trace of the former Mountain Ash Cardiff Road station (see page 26).

The sylvan surrounds and the high hills in the background belie the industrial nature of the area around Mountain Ash as Hudswell Clarke 0-6-0ST works No. 1885, NCB No. 1, gently manoeuvres wagons around the sidings at the north end of Deep Duffryn Colliery on a sunny 16 November 1973. The microphone held by the gentleman on the footplate was recording every sound emitted from the loco. The engine spent the first sixteen years of its existence from 1955 at Lady Windsor Colliery, Ynysybwl, before a transfer to Mountain Ash in July 1971. It was fitted with 18in. x 26in. cylinders, 4ft 0in. wheels and weighed 39 tons 8cwt. The large 'X' on the sides of the wagons denotes they were for use only on NCB lines. As the crow flies Merthyr Vale Colliery is only two miles away beyond the hills behind No. 1, but a journey of over eight miles, either by rail or road via Abercynon, where the waters of the Cynon merge with those of the Taff.

Opposite: With the gigantic Aberaman Phurnacite Plant forming a backdrop, ex-GWR Class 57XX 0-6-0PT No. 7754 bides time after hauling wagons up the valley from Mountain Ash on Sunday, 27 October 1974. The plant, which was developed by Powell Duffryn to produce smokeless briquettes for domestic consumption, became fully operational in 1942. At its peak it employed over 1,000 men and sold some one million tons of briquettes annually along with the by-products of tar, concentrated ammonia and gas for town use. The 200 Disticoke Inclined Ovens had to be fired constantly, the resultant pungent smelling atmospheric pollution being the subject of scores of complaints over the years. The plant was the only one of its kind. The history of No. 7754 is detailed on page 5.

Right: Later the same day No. 1 storms into the coal blending site near the old Cwmneol Colliery, Cwmaman, closed back in 1949. Noticeable is the missing dome cover, which was not replaced following some maintenance work at Lady Windsor Colliery prior to its move to Mountain Ash in 1971. The blending area was abandoned at the end of 1974 in favour of a much more convenient site near the phurnacite plant, not far from where No. 7754 was photographed opposite.

The rundown of the Mountain Ash Railway effectively started in September 1979 when mining ended at Deep Duffryn Colliery (although the washery was retained for a further twelve months). Then, three months later, on 28 December 1979 catastrophe struck when a torrential downpour caused the Cynon to burst its banks, flooding the railway at Mountain Ash, damaging one of the bridges and isolating the line south of the town. In consequence the conveyor that carried Penrikyber coal across the valley was rendered useless and the output from the colliery had perforce to revert to BR haulage. The next year proved the swansong for steam on the truncated system, 'Sir Gomer' being the last recorded turning a wheel early in December 1980. Little then changed until October 1985 when Penrikyber wound its last coal, the workshops at Mountain Ash being shut down the same year. The ovens at the phurnacite plant were finally extinguished in March 1990, much to the relief of many local households, the government refusing to invest further in the plant. On a more positive note, BR reinstated passenger services along the Cynon Valley in October 1988, enabling the residents of Mountain Ash to again travel direct to Cardiff or Aberdare along the old Taff Vale route.

Regarding the locomotives featured at Mountain Ash in these pages, remarkably all six were saved from an ignominious end at the hands of an uncaring scrap dealer. Today 'Llantarnam Abbey' and No. 8 remain companions on the Pontypool & Blaenavon Railway, while 'Sir John' resides on the Llanelli & Mynedd Mawr Railway at Cynheidre near Llanelli. Meanwhile, No. 7754 finds itself very much at home on former GWR metals at the Llangollen Railway in North Wales. The other two have both crossed the border into England, 'Sir Gomer' to the Battlefield Line, Shackerstone, Leicestershire, while No. 1 is on static display at the entrance to Fold House Caravan Park at Pilling, Lancashire. The latter masquerades as 'The Pilling Pig', as the engine that worked the former line between Garstang and Knott End was referred to by the locals.

Mardy Colliery at Maerdy (the colliery always used the anglicised version of the name) in the Rhondda Fach, was sunk under the direction of Brecon businessmen Wheatley Cobb and Mordecai Jones, the first coal being sold in 1877. As part of the construction work a two-mile railway was laid down the valley to Ferndale to connect with the Taff Vale Railway, the extension being taken over by the Taff Vale in 1886. Two years later the colliery was leased to Locket's Merthyr Steam Coal Co. Ltd, the sinking of No. 3 shaft, about one mile further up the valley from Nos. 1 & 2 shafts, commencing in 1893.

As Locket's Merthyr Collieries (1894) Ltd, the company remained independent until 1932 when its two pits (Mardy and Cilely at Tonyrefail) were acquired by Bwllfa & Cwmaman Collieries Ltd, a subsidiary of Welsh Associated Collieries Ltd. The same year Nos. 1 and 2 shafts were closed down, resources then being concentrated on Nos. 3 and 4 shafts, the latter dating from 1914. In 1935 Welsh Associated merged with the giant combine Powell Duffryn, Mardy subsequently being mothballed in 1940.

When the NCB became responsible for the coal industry in 1947, Mardy was one of ten pits in the Rhondda listed as 'not in production'. However this was soon to change, for during the early 1950s the NCB embarked on a massive £5 million investment scheme at Mardy, including a tunnel two and a half miles long to join the workings with those of Bwllfa Colliery in the Cwmdare Valley. The aim was to extract one million tons of coal per annum and provide employment for 2,800 men. In the event these ambitious targets were never realised; for example, in 1962, 399,000 tons were brought to the surface, the result of the labours of 1,606 men. During the early 1970s the pit sold approximately 250,000 tons each year, the employees numbering 1,125.

The bleak surroundings of the redeveloped colliery at Mardy, some 900 feet above sea level, are apparent in this photograph, taken on a dismal 8 October 1971. Peckett 0-6-0ST works No. 2150 'Mardy No. 1', built in 1954, shunts the sidings. In the centre foreground is a rail-mounted crane behind a Seddon Twin Ram Tipper, with one of the settling ponds to be seen on the right. The pipes alongside the service road carried water from a reservoir three miles further up the valley.

Not having turned a wheel for some three years, ex-Great Western Railway Class 57XX 0-6-0PT No. 9792, its number rather crudely painted on the side of the cab, looks in a rather woebegone state at the back of Mardy shed on 23 May 1973. The buffers, dome cover and cast number plates have already been removed. Released from Swindon Works in May 1936, the engine spent the first seven years of its existence attached to Brecon shed before moving to Neath in October 1943. It was withdrawn from the latter shed in March 1964 after completing over 500,000 miles, and sold the same month by BR to the NCB. Initially, it was used on the Aberaman Railway in the Cynon Valley before being transferred to Mardy early in 1965 where, nine years after its sale by BR, the engine still bears evidence of its former ownership. In addition to retaining its former number, its BR crest can be discerned through the grime on the side of the pannier tank. The letter 'C' superimposed on a yellow disc on the cab side sheet denoted its power classification and route availability when a main line engine. The cab side markings were originally introduced by the GWR, a system subsequently maintained by the Western Region of BR, the letter 'C' indicating it had a tractive effort in the 20,501lb. to 25,000lb. range, the yellow colouring confirming it could travel over all but the lightest of laid rails. A few weeks after this photograph was taken the engine was removed to the yard of James Mahoney & Co. Ltd at Newport Docks for scrapping.

Opposite: A panoramic vista of Maerdy taken from the B4277 mountain road from Aberdare on 7 October 1971. In the foreground 'Mardy No. 1' pulls away from the extensive sidings, built near the site of the original Nos. 1 and 2 shafts as part of the 1950s modernisation scheme, towards the colliery. Well over 200 wagons can be counted in the sidings. In the background are the slopes of Cefn y Rhondda which rise to 1,567 feet above sea level, while nestling below is the town of Maerdy, the older terraced houses being laid out to a grid pattern with some newer properties to the north and west. The former Maerdy station is just out of view to the left; passenger services from Porth were withdrawn in June 1964.

Below: A closer view of the hefty looking, work-stained 'Mardy No. 1', its name and works plates discarded, on 8 October 1971. It was popularly referred to as the 'Mardy Monster'. Peckett & Sons only put together three engines to this design, their Class OQ, which were the largest 0-6-0STs the firm ever built. The doyen, works No. 2124, was forwarded to Tower Colliery at Hirwaun in June 1951, with works No. 2150 going to Mardy in June 1954 and works No. 2151 following in September of the same year. In stark contrast to its appearance here, when 'Mardy No. 1' first set foot in South Wales it was resplendent in an azure blue livery with yellow and black lining, and the letters 'NCB' inscribed in gold paint on the centre panels of the saddle tank. Cast nameplates were attached to the cab side sheets above the works plates. Like its sisters, 'Mardy No. 1' had 18in. x 26in. outside cylinders, and 4ft 0½in. wheels. Tractive effort calculated at 85% of maximum boiler pressure of 200lb. was no less than 29,527lb. Thus the OQs were much more powerful than the other engines used at Mardy in later years, the Hunslet-designed 'Austerities' and No. 9792, which had nominal tractive efforts of 23,870lb. and 22,515lb. respectively. The OQs were also heavier than their counterparts at Mardy, turning the scales in full working order at 55 tons 0cwt., the 'Austerities' weighing 48 tons 5cwt. and No. 9792 49 tons 0cwt.

By the 1970s 'Mardy No. 1' was the only survivor of the class, the Tower engine having been scrapped in 1965 and 'Mardy No. 2' in 1968. It saw little use during the 1970s, diesels being preferred, and after a final steaming in the spring of 1976 lay idle until rescued in October 1979 and transported to the Swanage Railway. It stayed on the Dorset coast until April 1998 when it moved north to the Elsecar Steam Railway near Barnsley, where over a number of years it was painstakingly restored to working order again. It now rejoices officially under the name 'Mardy Monster'.

As for the colliery, the last coal was wound to the surface here on 30 June 1986, the final tub boldly inscribed 'Mardy Colliery Last Tram of Coal Raised in the Rhondda 30.6.86'. The coal was subsequently despatched by means of an underground conveyor via Tower Colliery. However, due to geological faults, by this time there was little life left in Mardy and it closed on 20 December 1990. This proved an emotional day, a large crowd gathering in the town before marching to the pit, where, after speeches, hymns and a rendering of 'Cwm Rhondda' by a brass band, they returned in procession behind a banner proudly borne aloft. Today, a tub of coal mounted on a brick plinth commemorates the closure of this the last of the fifty-three major collieries that once operated in the Rhondda. There is also a memorial in the form of a miniature headgear, which was dedicated by the Archbishop of Wales in June 1986 to the memory of the eighty-one men killed by an explosion at Mardy in December 1885.

Maesteg Central Washery was constructed by the NCB in 1957 on the site of the closed Maesteg Deep Colliery to process coal lifted from Caerau, Coegnant and St John's collieries (all owned prior to 1947 by North's Navigation Collieries (1889) Ltd), as well as some from other local mines. The aforementioned three collieries all worked the same seams underground, the combined output in 1962 amounting to 644,000 tons. During the early 1970s the railway system connecting the collieries with the washery was monopolised by Hunslet 'Austerity' 0-6-0STs, two being employed at the washery on the afternoon of 24 May 1973 when this photograph was taken. Works No. 3781, 'Linda', built in 1952, is reversing loaded wagons towards the screens, with works No. 3840, 'Pamela', built in 1956, to be glimpsed above the wagons on the right. Movements at the washery were controlled by colour light signals activated from the brick-built cabin visible above the wagon behind 'Linda'. A traverser (see page 19) was available at the back of the screens to transfer wagons between the various roads.

Photographed on 6 October 1971, Hunslet 'Austerity' loco 'Pamela' has arrived back at Maesteg Washery at the end of its two-mile journey from St John's Colliery, but requires a helping hand from its older sister 'Linda' to push the consist up the gradient to the back of the washery. A few minutes earlier 'Pamela' had hauled the load along the line on the left (see page 2), once part of the ex-Port Talbot Railway Port Talbot–Pontyrhyll route over which passenger services last ran in September 1932, although freight traffic continued until August 1964. The NCB then leased the section between Maesteg and Cwmdu sidings (where access was gained to St John's) from BR, over which successive colliery owners had in any case enjoyed running rights. Down the years the main line operating authorities always insisted on a brake van being attached to the rear of all mineral trains using the route, a practice that ceased after 1964. The semaphore signal on the left is a throwback to earlier days, when the route was part of the main line network. When 'Pamela' left Maesteg in June 1986, after spending the first thirty years of its life there, it did so as the last remaining steam locomotive on NCB soil in South Wales. Initially it was moved to the Vale of Neath Railway, but it is now at the Bridgend Valleys Railway, Pontycymer.

A separate branch, always privately owned, ran north from Maesteg Washery to Coegnant and Caerau collieries. 'Linda' is seen here engaged at the former on 24 May 1973. The cages attached to the winding wheels on the left lifted 120,000 tons of coal from up to 1,120 feet below the surface in 1947, a figure which increased to 229,000 tons in 1962, although by the early 1970s production had fallen to 180,000 tons per annum. During the 1970s, 750 men worked at the mine. The colliery closed due to geological problems in November 1981.

On the same day as the photograph opposite, having passed Coegnant Colliery 'Linda' heaves a set of sixteen empties, including five wooden-sided wagons, over an undulating section of track while on its way to Caerau Colliery. On this occasion, for some reason the shunter, ready to jump down when necessary to change the points, has chosen to ride in the second rather than the leading wagon. Perhaps he had found it easier to drop the side of the wooden wagon. The line in the left foreground connected with the ex-Great Western Railway Tondu–Abergwynfi line, just south of Caerau station, from which passenger services were withdrawn in July 1970, the route south being retained for the movement of coal. However, after being deprived of their train services for over twenty-two years, the citizens of Maesteg were pleased when these were reinstated in September 1992, even though only in the Bridgend direction.

A little later on 24 May 1973, having deposited the empties behind the screens in the background, 'Linda' departs from Caerau Colliery with the day's output at the start of its two and a half mile journey back to Maesteg Washery. The pit had been in production since the early 1890s. During 1947, 110,000 tons of coal passed over the colliery weighbridge, a similar figure being recorded in 1962, 601 men then depending on the mine for their wages, 505 toiling underground and 96 on the surface. In August 1977 Caerau became the first of the three collieries connected to Maesteg Washery to close.

Having run round the train seen opposite at Caerau, 'Linda' guides the seventeen wagons along the embankment at the approach to Maesteg Washery. The wagons at the lower level await collection by a BR Class 37 diesel locomotive, which will take them down the Llynfi Valley to Tondu and onwards to either Margam or Bridgend. Twelve years later the last coal raised from the former North's Navigation Collieries took place at St John's in November 1985. The washery remained busy until October 1989, after which it took until February 1993 to clear the accumulated stockpile of coal. Meanwhile diesel locomotives had been introduced to the colliery railway in June 1973, with 'Pamela' being retained as a spare in case of need. It was rarely called upon, with a last recorded steaming in January 1977. As regards 'Linda', like 'Pamela' (see page 39), after serving Maesteg from new it too has been preserved and is currently based on the Mid-Hants Railway at Alresford, near Winchester, where it has been converted to an 0-6-0T as a 'Thomas the Tank Engine' lookalike.

In 1872 coal was first brought out of Graig Merthyr Colliery, a drift mine (or slant, as they were known in South Wales) two miles north-east of Pontardulais in the remote Dulais Valley near the western extremity of the county of Glamorgan. The roadways, driven through hard sandstone, were unusual in that they needed no additional supports. Initially a 3ft 2in. gauge tramway linked the mine with Pontardulais, but this was replaced by a standard gauge railway in 1906. The steeply graded railway was the only viable means of access to this isolated outpost, and in 1947 some 215,000 tons of coal was hauled along its two and a half mile length to the main line exchange sidings just south of Pontardulais. By 1962 the output had increased to 277,300 tons. Over the years many of the miners regularly travelled to their place of work by 'Paddy' train, the usual formation being eight old vans fitted with bench seats, although in the mid 1950s a couple of ex-Great Western Railway compartment coaches of unknown vintage were acquired from BR. The last 'Paddy' trains ran in 1970, again using box vans. An unofficial duty for the engine crews was to deliver newspapers to a small farm and milk to a lineside cottage. Here, W.G. Bagnall-built 'Austerity' 0-6-0ST works No. 2758, with thirteen fully laden wagons from Graig Merthyr in tow, arrives back at Pontardulais on 24 May 1973. After completion in the builder's Castle Engine Works, Stafford, the engine was delivered as WD No. 75170 to the Ministry of Fuel & Power Upper Blaenavon opencast site in November 1944. It was employed thereafter at a number of such sites in South Wales before moving to Aberpergwm Colliery, Glyn Neath, in 1965. It was transferred to Pontardulais in July 1967.

Opposite: A few moments later, protected by a rather flimsy level crossing gate, the 'Austerity' crosses the main A48 Swansea–Carmarthen road as an MG Sports Model and a Ford Anglia behind wait to proceed in the Swansea direction. At one time miners clambered aboard the 'Paddy' trains just to the left of the crossing, but latterly a narrow platform was provided on the other side of the road by the engine shed.

45

Opposite: Two further views from 24 May 1973 at Pontardulais exchange sidings. These were connected to the former Great Western Railway Swansea avoiding line, although in pre-NCB days there had also been a link to the ex-London & North Western Railway route to Swansea Victoria. In the upper picture Bagnall works No. 2758 is again seen at work while (lower) fellow 'Austerity' Hunslet works No. 3770, 'Norma', built in 1952, shunts the sidings. 'Norma' had arrived at Pontardulais from Maesteg the previous February. On the left is one of the box vans formerly used on the 'Paddy' trains, retained as a mess hut.

Right: Mining was concluded at Graig Merthyr in June 1978, but activity at the BR exchange sidings continued for a further two years while a large stockpile of coal was cleared, most of it destined for Carmarthen Bay Power Station. However, only one engine was needed each day rather than two as previously. On 20 September 1979 Bagnall works No. 2758 simmers outside the small, one-road shed by the A48 at Pontardulais. The corrugated iron doors don't look too secure! To the right of the shed was a landsale yard. Both engines depicted on these two pages are still extant, 'Norma' now being maintained by the Cambrian Railways Society at Oswestry, while the Bagnall is a static exhibit at the Cefn Coed Colliery Museum at Crynant near Neath.

Brynlliw Colliery at Grovesend was located one mile south of Pontardulais. It was sunk by Thomas Williams (Llangennech) Ltd, production starting in 1908, but became a casualty of the harsh economic climate that prevailed after the First World War and lay dormant from 1925. In 1954 the NCB embarked on a major reconstruction scheme that took six years to complete at a cost of £4.8 million. By 1962 it employed 690 men with an output of anthracite coal totalling 337,400 tons, most of which was forwarded to local power stations. Here, veteran Peckett Class B2 0-6-0ST works No. 1426 rearranges the wagons at the busy landsale yard on 24 May 1973. The engine started its career with Glasbrook Bros Ltd, owners of Garngoch & New Gorseinon collieries at Gowerton, in November 1916. It stayed at Gowerton until moved the short distance to Brynlliw following closure of Garngoch in 1966.